HEARTWORK OF THE SOUL

YOUR TRAINING GUIDE TO EMOTIONAL WELLNESS

WORKBOOK

JOANNA AVIN

PURPOSE OF WORKBOOK

Thank you for investing in HeartWork® of The Soul. This workbook is the companion work to the information covered in the original narrative.

This workbook is designed to give you deeper insight into doing the HeartWork® of the heart. HeartWork® is the process of managing dormant or flared emotions to start the healing and restoration of one's soul. Doing the work is not an easy task, it requires faith, courage, and action.

Faith is the substance of things you are hoping for. Faith takes the outcome that you are looking for and brings it into your now. Faith is an intentional decision decided upon when fear is present. Fear tends to lurk until it drives our state of mind into a negative space, ultimately driving toxic behaviors. Fear seeks to paralyze our movements thus stagnating our progression. Sometimes we can be so close but feel so far away from our end goal. It's important to understand that everything that you need in this process is already before you, you just haven't physically experienced it. For example, going through the process of building our family homes, there were several building stages. I went to a contractor and discussed our needs. She took inventory of our specific requests and needs; then showed me a model home that resembled what I wanted in my finished home. I had a picture of the home to focus on throughout the process. When I met challenges and faced turmoil, I always kept the end in mind. While I was focusing on the end goal, contractors were clearing my lot, bringing the cinderblocks, wood, and other materials to the construction site at different times. I couldn't see every stage, but I always had a picture of the result. During this HeartWork® process, decide your result and keep that at the forefront of your mind. Don't allow the challenges through the process to redirect your decisions. Everything that was needed for our house was already there and even if I couldn't see the work, it didn't mean that things weren't working. I just had to have relentless faith and add courage.

Courage is the step that you take when fear decides it wants to handicap your movements. Courage laughs in the face of fear and does not allow fear to dictate rewriting your ending. Courage is difficult for many to embrace. However, on this journey of doing the HeartWork® it's pivotal to your success. Being courageous is also a choice, you must decide to have courage! Courage will shift your state of mind and move you from a limited mindset to a conquering mindset.

Building our home during the pandemic things got tough. Originally, we were told the house would be completed in six to nine months but that changed to almost two years! My landlord at the time was telling my family that we needed to move out immediately - but the house wasn't ready. I felt defeated, powerless, and extremely anxious. Where were we going to move? We needed our savings to continue paying for the new construction home in progress. As we looked through rental properties, landlords were asking for first and last month's rent, plus a security deposit. These payments combined were over seven thousand dollars! Fear was lurking all around and although I had the end picture in mind, my faith was failing. Gratefully, that was when I chose courage. We decided that we would look for an apartment instead of moving into another house. That was also the place where I had to partner my courage with action.

Action is an intentional aim to complete a process or thing. This is the area where many people fall short. They act impulsively or operate from a survival mindset. This is the time where one must weigh the data provided and move one step at a time. Many times, due to anxiety, many move in haste and regret their decisions. I decided that we would take a step back and eat the elephant one bite at a time. I began to research apartments and looked for what met our needs. I required a fair price, a good living space, and a location that was close to my kids' school. Gratefully, the waiting paid off and I was able to find an apartment (a transitional place) that met our requirements. My family and I stayed in the transition place for seven months, paid no penalty for breaking the lease early, and moved into our newly constructed home! Glory to God!

My hope is that as you go through the building process of your HeartWork® you will keep the faith, be courageous, and take the necessary actions. Always keep your end in mind. When challenged, decide to be courageous, and take one informed step at a time. Rinse and repeat as many times as necessary. Ultimately, you will build your new temple, where all the old was thrown away and you are showing up as a new creature. Ready, set, build!

HOW TO USE THIS WORKBOOK

This workbook has been uniquely designed for you. As a facilitator, I wanted to ensure that different types of learners would be able to engage and learn effectively. This workbook includes activities for understanding and retention, HeartWork® challenges for growth and development, note space for introspection, and testimonies to attest to the success of the life proven strategies provided.

The following are recommended guidelines:

- **Be honest with yourself**. You know yourself better than anyone and an open mind is needed for growth.

- **Prioritize yourself**. Set aside time to read and go through the activities at the same time. You get out of things what you put into them. Pastor Joel Tudman says, "If you want to win big you have to have big input."

- **Commit to completing each challenge.** Each HeartWork® challenge will be difficult, however, your victorious self is worth the work.

- **Get an accountability partner**. Accountability partners will ensure that you love yourself in a way that brings about significant change. Choose someone who will speak to you in love and has your best interest at heart.

Provide them with the dates and times you will complete certain chapters or assignments and allow them to hold you to these timelines.

- **Celebrate yourself**. Completing this work can get emotionally exhausting. Make time to treat yourself to relaxation and peace. You will need it.

CONTENTS

INTRODUCTION

To begin the journey of doing the HeartWork® you must begin to design your blueprint.

What are some areas that you are looking to improve upon?

____

____

____

Now that you have identified those areas, which attributes are you looking to embrace and walk in? These answers help to determine your success blueprint.

____

____

____

PART I

Are You Feeling Some Type of Way?

PUTTING IT ALL TOGETHER

Think back to a recent conflict with a friend, loved one, or co-worker. Diagram 1 is our reference point for this exercise. Write down what information was coming in through your five senses.

Diagram 1

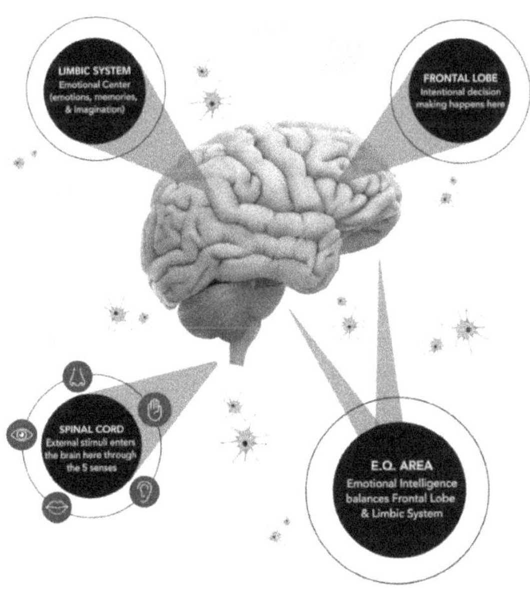

SIGHT – What did your physical eyes see as you were in conflict with that individual?

____

____

____

SOUND – What sounds did you hear?

____

____

____

TOUCH – What were you touching?

____

____

____

SMELL – What did you smell?

____

____

____

The information that came through your senses happened in milliseconds and now you are feeling some type of way. What emotions did you feel when that individual did not agree with your perspective?   15

____

____

____

While you are feeling some type of way (feeling angry, irritated, frustrated, etc.), your emotions are telling you that you must do something about the conflict. What were your actions as a result of those demanding emotions? How did you feel twenty-four hours later?

____

____

____

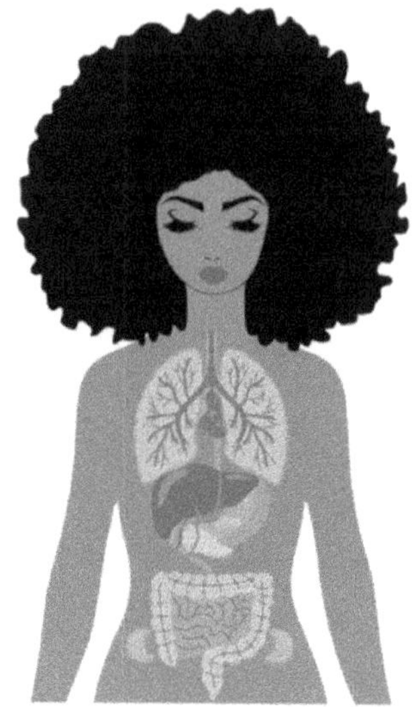

Imbalances in emotions can lead to illnesses in their corresponding organs.

LUNGS	LIVER	KIDNEYS	HEART	INTESTINES	GALLBLADDER
Anxiety Sadness	Anger Fear	Fear	Anxiety Fear Happiness Sadness Surprise Thoughtfulness	Fear Anxiety Worry	Fear Surprise

Our emotions directly impact our brain and other parts of the body. Other than the internal organs listed in Diagram 2, I want you to do more research. What other areas of your body are impacted by your emotions (for example, digestive system, immune system, circulatory system, etc.)?

____

____

____

REVIEW: ARE YOU FEELING SOME TYPE OF WAY?

1. Almost _________ of your decisions are based on your brain operating on autopilot.
2. Information enters our spinal cord through our _________, _________, _________, _________, and _________.
3. The _________ is located in the limbic system and is responsible for storing memories and emotions.
4. Our _________ is responsible for our rational thinking. This area of our brain allows us to think about the long- and short-term consequences of our behavior.
5. _________ _________ occurs when decisions are made without engaging the frontal lobe.

Key Points

- HeartWork® is the process of managing dormant or flared emotions to start the healing and restoration of one's soul.

- There is no scientific evidence that supports that women are more emotional than men. – According to the National Institute of Health.

- Emotions are energy in your feelings that drive you to or away from action.

- Unresolved or suppressed emotions from childhood will impact your decision making as an adult.

- A person's Emotional Quotient is more valuable than one's Intelligence Quotient.

- Awareness and intentionality to incorporate better practices concerning your health is pivotal in maintaining a healthier body.

MOMENTS OF INTROSPECTION

What awarenesses did you gain after reading this chapter?

PART II

Are you Babysitting Spinach?

EMOT-SUN® VOCABULARY

We learned that an estimated 50 percent of the time we make decisions on autopilot. One of the first things we must be intentional about is identifying our current state of mind. Unfortunately, many are not aware of the emotional vocabulary for expression. The Emot-Sun® Diagram, (Diagram A3) provides an array of additional emotions that we experience but rarely communicate.

HeartWork® Challenge

Think about a difficult conversation that you need to have with someone. Use the Emot-Sun® Diagram and identify what you are currently feeling just thinking about having the conversation? How do you think you may feel after you have had the conversation? Write your responses below.

Emotions prior to conversation:

____

Expected emotions after conversation:

____

Now, that you completed the pre-work for your conversation. The next challenge is for you to have that difficult conversation and not allow fear to paralyze your actions. Record the results of that conversation below.

____

____

____

TESTIMONY CORNER

I've had many challenging conversations through my emotional healing journey. As I began doing the hard work of the heart, I was faced with scenarios where I needed to practice what I preached. I had been working for a company about four years, when my manager was laid off and I was under consideration for Training Manager. I was excited and eager to begin this new role. I was already responsible for the training and development of about 50-70 in-house representatives, and I had two employees who reported directly to me. When my previous manager was laid off, the three of us worked diligently and closely to ensure a strong and cohesive unit. We discussed our thoughts concerning the possible management opening position. Both of my co-workers decided they were not interested in the position for various reasons. However, I was interested and eager to show my skill set to the leadership team. I worked tirelessly on several projects, staying late, working from home, to deliver on my objectives. In the end, my hard work paid off and I was promoted. To celebrate I took my new team out to lunch, and we discussed my new role and the vision for the training department. The next day I got to work; Human Resources called me into the office. They received a complaint from my team that I made inappropriate statements to them during lunch. I was completely caught off guard and mortified by the news. I was instructed that I needed to speak with my team and get their buy-in or the new position would be over. Ugh…ugh… ugh….are you kidding me?! I didn't even want to look at my team after I got the news. I felt betrayed, irritated, and disgusted by their actions. Why couldn't they just come to me if I said anything that may have offended them? But I had to choose to have the difficult conversation and rise above my emotions. I decided to meet with them individually and talk through their discomfort during our lunch together. This was an exceedingly difficult conversation, but I had to lay aside my pride and do the work. After meeting with each of them and discussing the issues, I apologized and assured them I would be more conscious of my actions and words moving forward. After the conversation, I felt relieved, empowered, and we had come to a mutual understanding of how we would proceed moving forward. This was just one of many challenging conversations I've had over the years. I encourage you to begin having more difficult conversations. I grew tremendously in my awareness of handling conflict with others. Going through the experience I wouldn't change anything.

SELF-ASSESSMENT

Awareness includes recognizing, identifying, and understanding how you show up and affect others every day.

HeartWork® Challenge: Conflict is inevitable. We will encounter conflict in all areas of our life (work, home, school, etc.) This challenge will help you manage your emotions prior to an eruption. Write down three strengths and three areas of opportunity in your character during conflict

STRENGTHS

____

____

____

AREAS OF OPPORTUNITY

____

____

____

Next, ask a family member, friend, and a co-worker to list three strengths and three areas of opportunity for you during conflict.

FAMILY MEMBER

____

____

____

FRIEND

____

____

____

CO-WORKER

____

____

____

Look at the feedback that you received from your family and friends and locate any consistent areas in your strengths and opportunities. After you have identified those areas, look at the feedback that you wrote concerning yourself. Was there consistency between the feedback that you provided for yourself and the feedback from your family and friends, and if not, what were the areas that were inconsistent? These areas indicate the spinach that you may have missed or have not made necessary adjustments in your character to address. Write those areas down for future work.

____

____

____

TRIGGERS

Self-awareness also requires having a level of patience to dig into places within yourself that may be uncomfortable. A trigger is something that someone can do or say that can immediately cause you to feel an intense emotion. The intensity of this emotion can cause you to say or do things quickly without thinking about the short- or long-term impacts of your behavior. So, let's explore this together.

HeartWork® Challenge: Think about three triggers in conflict that can immediately cause you to get angry, sad, depressed, etc. and write them down.

TRIGGER:

____

____

____

I also want you to begin the drill down process of finding the root of this trigger. How do you find the root? Begin to ask yourself why and what may have caused this attitude. For example, you have identified that when people lie to you, you immediately feel frustrated, irritated, and angry. Ask yourself why do you get so angry? What is causing those feelings? What is the first memory that you can think of in which someone older lied to you and you couldn't do anything about it, so you suppressed the emotion?

Write that name down

____

REVIEW: ARE YOU BABYSITTING SPINACH?

1. Name the six primitive emotions that are with us from birth __________, __________, __________, __________, __________, __________.

2. The Emot-Sun Diagram provides the __________ to express how you are feeling for accuracy.

3. Emotions cannot be destroyed only transferred or __________.

4. According to your HeartWork® Challenge Assessment, which conflict area will you begin to work on first and how?

____

____

____

5. Set a date to speak with the person in which you are in conflict and inform your accountability partner. Write your date below.

____

Additional Notes

- Show up for your family better than how you treat your co-workers. Be intentional about demonstrating patience, kindness, and grace. Your family will be there for you when an employer terminates your position.

- Expressing one's emotions is not a sign of weakness but a sign of strength and character. Articulating what's in the heart brings truth and ultimately freedom. Emotions must be expressed, or they will begin to create pockets in your soul that will ultimately recycle pain and abuse to oneself and others.

- Psychologist Dr. Travis Bradberry completed a study that indicates that we are only able to identify and recognize what we are feeling in the moment 34 percent of the time.

- Self-awareness is a process that will continually prove itself to you. As you continue doing your work, you will receive a window of grace that will appear prior to you falling back into a toxic pattern.

MOMENTS OF INTROSPECTION

What awarenesses did you gain after reading this chapter?

____

____

____

____

____

____

____

____

____

____

____

____

____

____

____

____

____

____

What awarenesses did you gain after reading this chapter?

PART III

Get it Togetha

MANAGING NEGATIVE THOUGHTS

Managing disruptive thoughts, emotions, and impulses takes HeartWork®. This work is not easy and requires an open mind and attentiveness to the process. One major contaminator to becoming free of obtrusive and harmful thoughts is our self-talk. Several types of self-talk have been researched but I am going to discuss four types that I have personally experienced.

1. Brain Reading: You assume that you know what people are going to think, even though you don't have enough evidence about their thoughts.

2. Fortune-telling: You think you can predict the future and that everything will be worse or something dangerous will happen.

3. Labeling: You have subconscious negative opinions about yourself or others. You claim that the positive things you or others have or have achieved are insignificant.

4. Negative filter: You'll focus on anything negative that could happen. You become so consumed by this narrative that you build damaging thoughts, forgetting that good could come out of the situation.

HeartWork® Challenge

Think about the previous HeartWork® Challenge, where you set a date to speak with an individual with whom you have conflict.

Write the person's name

Begin to think about the conflict and determine if the conflict was based on a possible different upbringing, culture, religion, or life experiences (trauma)?

Write the root of the conflict.

As you set the date to have the conversation, which negative self-talk surfaced?

HeartWork® Challenge

Each time I get to teach Emotional Intelligence (EI), I challenge participants to begin the process of healing their triggers. Below are steps that will empower you to release the energy that can ultimately cause damage to you internally.

1. *Write a letter.* In Part II, you worked through getting to the seed of your trigger. Grab a pen and paper or a device that can capture your thoughts. Recall the memory that caused an emotion to emerge. Sit with yourself and begin to write down your thoughts and express the areas in which you were unable to release previously. Use the Emot-Sun Wheel to identify and articulate the emotions that will arise. Explain in the letter how their actions impact your behaviors as an adult. Use this as an opportunity to get it all out, in love and with kindness.

2. *Forgive yourself and the seed of your trigger. Forgiveness is one of the keys that unlocks the hardness of the heart.* Forgiveness also releases the emotions that have been explosive when your buttons are pushed. Many times, we think that if we forgive people, we are letting them off the hook and they need to pay for what they did to us. However, forgiveness does not let them off the hook but lets you off the hook to live a healed life.

3. *Read the letter to the seed of your trigger.* This is a tremendously difficult step. I've heard of people trying to manage unforgiveness by making a list of the people that they need to forgive and saying, "I forgive you" to each name listed. Unfortunately, this strategy does not convert or transfer the internal energy. Allowing yourself to go back to the

memory, feel the emotion, and speak while expressing the emotion allows for a healthy conversion. I'm going to challenge you to read your letter to the person at the root of your seed. This is where the negative thoughts will begin to overwhelm your mind. The mission of those thoughts is to keep you in internal pain; but don't give in. Reading the letter converts the stored energy that you are feeling (weak, anxious, or insecure) and allows you to feel strengthened, encouraged, and relieved.

4. *If the seed of your trigger is deceased,* complete the first two steps. The only difference is that you will read your letter to a proxy who will stand in the gap for the deceased individual. Choose someone that you trust and thinks good thoughts about you. Set a time and date and release your words.

Write the name of the seed of your trigger.

____

Write Your Letter.

____

____

____

____

____

____

____

*Bonus HeartWork® Challenge

I found it very difficult to move through my life because of the thoughts that I felt towards myself. During my life I've felt rejected, unloved, stupid (which isn't a feeling but I'm using it as one), embarrassed, etc. and the list can go on and on. It was hard for me to accept that I was qualified to receive good things and accolades from others. I felt like an imposter. If people only knew what I was truly made of they would surely reject me. I wallowed in this misery for years wearing a mask. I finally found the answer that would lift this weight of insecurity off my heart. I decided to write myself a letter. I wrote down decisions that were humiliating, embarrassing, and unloving. I identified the emotional vocabulary that was tied to each decision, and I decided to forgive myself and begin operating from a victorious mindset. I chose a person that I knew would support and care for me and I read the letter to them. The weight that was lifted off my shoulders was truly indescribable. This practice created a window of awareness that appeared prior to making a decision that resembled a victimized mindset. Day after day my strength grew, and I began loving myself in a way that I had never experienced before. I want you to experience this love towards yourself.

HeartWork® Challenge

Write a letter to yourself and include the areas in which you feel the most embarrassed or angry with yourself. Identify the emotional vocabulary that is lying underneath and choose someone that will allow you the space to read the letter to them.

Write Your Letter

REVIEW: GET IT TOGETHA

1. _________________ is defined as controlling your disruptive moods or behaviors in the moment.
2. Your emotions act as an _________________, to provide you safety and security prior to an eruption.
3. _________________ is the type of self-talk in which you assume that you know what people are going to think even though you don't have enough evidence about their thoughts.
4. _________________ is the type of self-talk which generates subconscious negative opinions about yourself or others.
5. As a man thinketh in his _________________, so is he.

Key Points

- Chinese Philosopher Lao Tuz said, "Watch your thoughts; they become words. Watch your words; they become actions. Watch your actions; they become a habit. Watch your habits; they become character. Watch your character; it becomes your destiny."
- *Thoughts are powerless until you begin to believe them and give them life by picking them apart.* You have a choice, whether you will succumb to your thoughts and allow them to dictate your life or choose to speak what's true and hopeful
- *Focus on the things that you can control.* Attempting to control others is a waste of time, energy, and effort. The only person you can truly control is yourself.
- Never allow the emotional reaction of someone else to dictate your response or actions.
- Commit to taking the HeartWork® Letter Challenge and having that difficult conflict conversation.

*Bonus Content

Affirmations are pivotal in maintaining a positive state of mind. Affirmations are positive statements that you repeat to yourself to challenge negative thoughts and cultivate a more optimistic outlook. Challenging thoughts are crucial since 95% of our thoughts are subconscious and 80% of those thoughts are negative – According to the National Science Foundation.

HeartWork® Challenge

Repeat the following affirmations whenever you are in a defeated state of mind. Speak them aloud and experience the results of your intentionality.

- I release the troubles and worries from yesterday and embrace the opportunities of the day because I am loved by God.
- I am courageous and confident in who I am, and in my abilities, because I am loved by God.
- I lack nothing and no-thing will be held from me because I am loved by God.
- I have complete wellness in my body, soul, and spirit because I am loved by God.
- I am successful in everything that I touch because I am loved by God.
- Nothing I face will ever defeat me; I stay victorious because I am loved by God.
- I am grateful, thankful, and blessed because I am loved by God.
- I have knowledge, wisdom, and patience to make wise decisions because I am loved by God.

- I will not allow my present troubles to dictate my future self because I am loved by God.
- I have peace and clear vision for my future because I am loved by God.
- My business/job and finances are blessed because I am loved by God.
- Any trauma, hurt, or pain is redeemed because I am loved by God.
- I speak life over my children and my children's children because I am loved by God.
- I render every toxic generational pattern powerless because I am loved by God.
- I take authority over any and every act of witchcraft or sorcery over me and my family because I am loved by God.
- I release divine protection and healing over me and my family because I am loved by God.
- I call forth divine connections to me because I am loved by God.
- I find rest in the shadow of the Almighty because I am loved by God.
- I release generational wealth over my children and my children's children because I am loved by God.
- I receive everything that God has for me before the foundation of the world, because I am loved by God.
- And most importantly, I am proud of myself and love myself because God first loved me.

MOMENTS OF INTROSPECTION

What awarenesses did you gain after reading this chapter?

PART IV

Sick and Tired of Being
Sick and Tired

HeartWork® Challenge

Write three short term goals and three long term goals. Ensure that the short-term goals align with your long-term goals. Determine the steps that you must take to get to your desired result. For example, I had to commit to going to the gym, focus on my nutrition, and face the scale for accountability every week. What measures can you set up to ensure you achieve your goals?

Short Term Goals (3-6 months)

____

____

____

Long Term Goals (6 months-3 years)

____

____

____

Who is your accountability partner and what date will you begin your short-term goals?

REVIEW: SICK AND TIRED OF BEING SICK AND TIRED?

1. True or False, Motivation is an emotion or general desire.
2. _____________ is defined as control gained by enforcing obedience or order, demonstrating self-control·
3. __________ _____________ said, "You miss 100% of the shots you don't take."
4. Taking _________ is the power that will fuel your action regardless of others.
5. _______________________________________, is the acronym for fear, according to Bishop TD Jakes, Founding Pastor of The Potter's House, Dallas, Texas.

Key Points

- Win the war internally by taking initiative, setting goals, and being committed to your process.
- Discipline strategies that can assist you on your journey.
  - Awareness – Identify the obstacles that prevented you from completing your goal previously. Drill down to understand the root reason and shift your attitude.
  - Regulate - Set measurable goals with timelines and include an accountability partner. Goals must be specific, attainable, and include dates that coincide with each milestone.
  - Celebrate your results. Take the time to think of ways you can reward yourself after each milestone. Prioritize your wants and be proud of your accomplishments.

- ○ Self-Assessment. During the journey of achieving your goal set a time to re-evaluate or recalibrate your results. Determine what went well, what can be improved, and how to execute it more effectively in the future.

MOMENTS OF INTROSPECTION

What awarenesses did you gain after reading this chapter?

____

____

____

____

____

____

____

____

____

____

____

____

____

____

____

____

____

____

____

PART V

Are You Really Sorry to Hear That?

HeartWork® Challenge

Create three empathetic statements below. Here's the situation, you are calling to check on a friend who you haven't heard from in a while. After speaking with her for a few moments, she shares that she has been feeling overwhelmed and depressed because her 12-year-old dog passed away. How would you respond to her. Write your statements below.

____

____

____

HeartWork® Challenge

When you fall short of your goal, what will you do differently based on the information that you have learned about yourself?

____

____

____

REVIEW: ARE YOU REALLY SORRY TO HEAR THAT?

1. According to Brene Brown, ____________ is a skill that can bring people together and make people feel included, while ____________ creates an uneven power dynamic and can lead to more isolation and disconnection.
2. To connect with others, the work begins in the ____________ first. You must place yourself in another person's shoes.
3. Empathy does not seek to ____________ the person or situation but seeks to ____________ and relate with them in the moment.
4. When people are in an ____________ ____________ state of mind, connecting with others can help alleviate some of the stress of their situation and allow for emotions to be processed
5. Be aware that your ____________ and view of a situation is not the only or best perspective.

Key Points

- Patience is defined as one's capacity to accept or tolerate delay, trouble, or suffering without getting angry or upset.
- Grace is undeserved favor and is not something that is earned but freely given.
- Mercy is having compassion or forgiveness shown toward someone when it is within one's power to punish or harm them.
- Slow down your thoughts and actions and take a deep breath. Intentionality allows you to engage the frontal

lobe and make a decision that has not been emotionally hijacked.

- Create the disciplines of opening your heart, being vulnerable, and trusting people again. It is time to let go of the weighty emotional baggage and live again.

MOMENTS OF INTROSPECTION

What awarenesses did you gain after engaging this workbook and what information will you share with others?